Rachel's Realm - A Portal of Witches' Wisdoms.

Rachel Baker

Presentation by *BookLeaf Publishing*

Web: www.bookleafpub.com

E-mail: info@bookleafpub.com

ISBN: 9789357617796

First edition 2022

I would like to dedicate this little book to my family - my Mother, (my best friend) Father, Brother and Son xx. I love you all so so much.

Adin - thank you for saving my life. Literally. I love you.

Jorg - thank you for the journey of my soul. I know it was you . My heavenly saviour. I love you.

ACKNOWLEDGEMENT

I would like to thank my life experiences, pathways chosen, destinations encountered and people I've met so far whilst having this Earth experience. Anything in my past that may have occurred slightly differently would not have seen me standing where I am today. Some occurances have not yet revealed their meaning as to "why" certain encounters played out the way they did, yet so many have so far in my life. I believe everything that happens to you, happens for a reason, which does end up revealing itself as to why. Take each experience as a lesson or a blessing. Learn from each one. Let your soul evolve from each lesson learnt. Feel the emotions and sit with them. Remember that emotion only sits with you for a time. Don't wait to feel happiness, be happy within yourself. It's not a destination, it's all about the journey within ❤

PREFACE

Most of these poems seem to have written themselves, with myself just pushing the pen. From the calls I hear in nature, to the secrets whispering in the winds, I see it written. Whether moon manifesting, conjuring magick with intentions, reading history on the atrocities carried out on our sisters of time ago - the words create the theme and sing in my mind, until jotted down and splayed onto paper for eyes to read. Almost lyrical, always intentional, forever magickal. I hope this book sits with you on rainy days and quiet moments, and fills a part of your soul, or stirs an awakening inside that has been fast asleep. Encapture the essence, feel the beauty, feed the witch. X

The Magick In The Day.

Before my eyes were open, before the "rise and
shine",
a melancholy memory set a stage inside my
mind.
It played a haunting sadness-
this memory of dread.
Like a song or tune you hum all day
that gets stuck in your head.

I went outside to see the day,
my thoughts were filled with fear.
I turned around to go back in -
didn't notice what was near.

A gentle breeze was blowing,
coming off the backyard creek,
I didn't see the gift as I had slowly turned my
cheek.

A perfect white birds'; feather being carried with
the wind,
had landed where my feet had been and nooked
itself right in.

It was a gift of many - but I had turned away.

I'd failed to see the first sign of the magick in
the day.

I made my bed and showered- gave the house a
little love,
I hadn't seen the windowsill that graced a
gorgeous dove.
This messenger of goddess watch me close, then
flew away.
I'd missed the second gift that was the magick in
the day.

I thought that I was over it - this haunting from
the past.
My head so deep in shadows with those
memories playing fast.
My routine out of whack today, my conscience
hitting hard.
Would have flipped the suit of pentacles had I
drawn my daily card.

No meditation for my soul, no nature walks
away,
I'd missed the third and fourth signs that held
magick in the day.

I ran some errands, shopped for food,
half conscious from afar.

Didn't even hear my favourite song whilst
driving in the car.
I put the food away at home then went into my
room,
I'd missed the fact my latest plant had flowered
to full bloom.
I closed my eyes, sat on the floor, my thoughts
just wouldn't sway,
I'd missed the fifth and sixth signs that gave
magick to the day.

Then something hit me slowly, a wave of stoic
truth.
My thoughts and fears had stole my day! My
innocence! My youth !
My precious time was wasted in a struggle for
today!
My consciousness had failed to see the magick
in the day!

To close a book, you have to look within and
hold it true.
To feel - then heal emotions that were making
you so blue.
Then let it go - not hold it in, just send it on its
way.
Your life won't last stuck in the past,
a sad lesson to pay.

Stay in the now and living, not behind or future being.
Live every single moment conscious true and conscious seeing.
Don't ever swap your "now and here" - be aware now if it strays,
or you won't see signs from Divine -
The Magick In The Day ♥

Stardust.

Do you wish upon a star?
Do you believe its true -
that if you catch it falling it could be good luck
for you?
What's the first thing you would wish for?
Popularity and wealth?
Or would you wish on deeper things,
like happiness and health?

Perhaps your wish contained a plea -
a wish for peace on Earth.
A bandaid big enough to fit around our Gaia's
girth.

Do you ever spare a moment for your
empathetic soul?
To walk barefoot on soft green grass and make
yourself feel whole?

Or do you stay in "flight or fight " -
unable to unwind,
expecting any second is the end for all mankind
?

Are you the great protector for the ones you love
so dear?
You take the brunt to shield your tribe,
to spare them of the fear.

Or when you're out in public, do you feel like
you could drown?
You wonder if there's others like yourself that's
still around.

You feel a shift of energies-
you feel you don't belong.
Your feet are dancing to the tune
of an unfamiliar song.

You find yourself engaging less in media and
news,
and watch the sunset in the skies and marvel in
the hues.

The turmoil and uncertainty can leave you in a
spin.
Remember- reconnect yourself. Sit silent. Go
within.
The sentient awareness of your being is not a
curse.
We're placed around the world
and now we're ready to disperse.

We're here to guide and heal the folk who don't
know how to be,
at one with self and fellow man,
to help them all to see.

For they too would have sat at night and wished
upon a star,
and made their wish for fortunes or that big new
shiny car.
And we can guide them to a thought -
their higher self will reign.
Connection to the universe is what they will
attain.

For we have stardust in our blood,
it makes us who we are.
It's in the plants, the animals -
we're remnants of the stars.

Don't wait to see a shooting star to pledge your
wishes from afar.
Just shout it out - be loud and true -
for the universe is me and you. ❤

Gaia.

I watched her for a while today
and safely took her in -
As my hair is long enough
to veil my face and hide within.

She moved like liquid silver,
so sleek and maiden fair.
Her beauty undeniable
with golden auburn hair.

Upon her lips of scarlet red,
her laughter filled the space.
Her smile a ray of beacon light
upon her gorgeous face.

The way she told her stories
was enchanting in itself.
They gathered round to hear her speak
and gaze upon her wealth.

The children love her dearly,
was a pleasure to be seen.
The young and old alike
encaptured by her eyes of green.

I stay still in the shadows,
I hold my breath within.
I long to speak to her but don't know where I
would begin.

Her long and slender fingers
hold great magick to be seen.
She makes the rivers run again-
the flora evergreen.

The brightness in the mornings.
The dark days hold no fear.
The love and light is felt by all whenever she is
near.

And when you need her magick,
she'll be there to take your hand.
To restore faith and love again across all of the
lands.

She sees me now- she's smiling as she walks to
my embrace.
The essence of divinity worn on her pretty face.

She knows how much I love her.
She knows I hold her true.
Her energies and aura glowing with a golden
hue.

She's elements. She's thunderstorms.
She whispers through the trees.
Her voice is carried gently in the travels of a
breeze.

She's beautiful. She's passionate,
yes - we all know her worth.
She's always been, and always will -
She's GAIA - Mother Earth

The Hill. (Based around the tragedies of the trials of the Pendle "witches", Lancaster, England. - Year 1612. NEVER FORGOTTEN.)

Long ago, when times were poor,
she came a knocking on my door.
Our first encounter- not the slightest our last,
was when the first ancestry ties were cast.

The knock was hurried, urgent, loud.
Her stance was rigid, present, proud.
Her hair was wild, her clothes were worn.
A sight to see at early dawn.

My eyes snapped open, my body rose.
My focus still foggy from restful repose.
I neared my door- then composed my own state,
then swung it right open to face my ill fate.

"Well you took your time," she rudely had said.
"For a moment I thought that perhaps you were dead.
I've come to ask for a favour as such.

Oh don't look like that- it isn't too much."

As I processed the moment and took it all in,
my eyes fell to stare at three hairs on her chin.
An old crone apparent, and set in her ways.
Her light though- was shining, and fully ablaze.

"Yes, I may look old with this curve in my back,
but my wit is still perfect and sharp as a tack.
My visions have led me here straight to your
door,
for you';re the young lady that I'm looking for."

"Well I hope I can help then," I started to say,
as she entered my home and pushed me out the
way.
"We must hurry dear, there's no time to spare,
come sit in here with me and pull up a chair.
If you have any questions, please leave them till
last.
Take notes when you can, for I speak very fast."

She erupted in tales of wisdom and lore.
The heartache and torture of our sisters before.
And then her face softened- her eyes cast a
glaze.
A tear shed in memory of torturous days.

"My mother you see, was a threat if you will.

She was one of the 12 "witches" from Pendle
Hill."

My eyes must have widened, for she nodded her
head.
"Could you have imagined their fear and their
dread?
There was bad blood among them, but how
could they guess,
that their youngest would stop to bow down and
"confess?"
One hanged at York Assizes, one passed from
her ill.
Nine others left hanging upon Pendle Hill.

Which leads me to tell you, come as it may-
of one who was spared- her name Alice Grey.
They found her not guilty, her hanging was
spared.
She had lived to tell her tale if she had so dared.

Alice Grey was my mother, in fact, she had two.
Yes, I had a sister, and she then had you.
So I'm your Aunt Winnie, the one who had run
away from society when trouble begun.

I'd not seen your mother for many turns of the
tide.
I left it too late when I heard she had died.

Then I learnt about you, and made it my quest,
to meet my dear niece- of whom she'd loved
best."

To which I then smiled and said "Winnie, it's
true!
The crafts' in our blood- it's in me, and in you.
We'll cast a great circle and hold to us dear,
our sisters condemned from afar and from near.
We'll honour their names and remember them
still,
the "witches" whose souls rest, upon Pendle
Hill."

The Prize.

When you shed your own skin from that person
before,
and discover a new realm behind a closed door,
it's easy to think you are losing your mind,
as your friends and old life just start lagging
behind.....

You come to the door, but you just want to keep
your life as you know it- but you then take a peep.
Once seen, you cannot remain in your old ways.
Your nights become sleepless, then stretch into days.

As your mindset evolves and your values all change,
you welcome the "mystical," the "different," the
"strange."
You find inner knowing- your spiritual soul.
You uncover hard truths down in that rabbithole.

You then meet your ego, and your shadow self.
Emotions connected to physical health.
Your thought patterns making your life as you know.
Your "Dark Night " played out like some grim horror
show.

Observing behaviours of others without
your opinion on what their life is all about.
No competition- no "better than you."
No eyes judging everything that they may do.

Material things are no longer the prize,
it's replaced by compassion and love in ones' eyes.
It's how you help others and help them to heal,
then lead them to see that "attraction " is real.

"Like attracts like " - our thoughts manifest,
into lives that we live- that we love- or detest.
"Nature abhors a vacuum" - (A true empty space.)
Fill those empty cups right up with kindness and
grace.
"The present is always perfect" - well, no it is not?
Know imperfect IS perfect, with all that we've got.

Three Laws of Attraction to create your good life,
with abundance aplenty, and good fortune runs rife.
Turn up your vibration, let your frequency speak.
Make your voice grab attention whenever you speak.

They'll listen with new truths now set in their hearts.
They'll lead and show others the place where to start.
They'll talk of the one who had let it all go,
stepped out of the comfort zone that we all know.

She's the one who was fearless and didn't look back,
as she quit the dead life and she made a new track.
It's path was not walked upon- destination unknown.
So she followed her heart with new seeds she had
sown.

And what she discovered, is what she now knows,

through the tears of confusion where doubts like to grow.
Through learning and wisdom, through silence and stealth,
she discovered the prize- and that was herself. ❤

Witch Trials - Part 1 - The Beginning of the End. (Loosely based around true events)

One would have thought that they'd just let her be,
after cutting her down from the limbs of a tree.
Her wrists red and bruising from rope that was bound -
her face scratched and bleeding from hitting the ground.

As she lay there, she conjured her next civil move.
Her innocence still stood as something to prove.
If she were to move quickly, she'd startle them all.
No-one here to help her, no name she could call.

The smell of charred fabric lay thick in the air.
Her clothes had been burnt, as well as her hair.
She slowly stood up, with her head still bowed low.
Her postural sway moving from to and fro.

There stood about twenty - she'd counted their
heads, as they'd shouted profanities and wanted
her dead.
These men were barbaric with their torturous
ways.
They'd burn you alive- leave you hanging for
days.

They would torture the women who were seen
as a threat,
and accuse them of witchcraft every chance they
would get.
Medicine women, and healers as well,
were considered as evil spawned straight down
in hell.

Knowledge or beauty was a threatening trait -
you'd be lynched and then tortured, securing
your fate.
Nurses or midwives, plant medicine brews,
were all seen as witchcraft, "what evil would
do."

All single women had intentions impure.
They'd lead you astray with seductive allure.

And if you were gifted with a beautiful face,
an hourglass figure and a temperament of grace -

You're a sorceress, a vixen, leaving all men
"spellbound,"
"It wasn't his fault if he chased you around!"

Which is why her confusion of them cutting her
down,
caused a feel of uncertainty, had her face in a
frown.
From the crowd he emerged, and then spat at her
feet.
She saw him and instantly went white as a sheet.

'Twas he that caused her to be up on display.
He had made advances- and she hadn't played.
His ego was hurt - his manhood denied.
He accused her of sorcery - convicted and tried.

As he gazed her over, his smile was obscure.
She wondered what next she would have to
endure.

We've made a decision, a mutual pact.
You'll be trialled under law known as the
"Witchcraft Act."
It's punishable by death as you probably have
guessed,
but first you must pass a few witch trial tests.

You won't be alone, you'll have plenty of peers.

You'll be put in the jails till you face all your
fears.
We will see just how many of you pass the tests.
I'm sure for your life you'll convince us your
best."

He led her towards the great holding cell,
as her breath caught her throat which had started
to swell.
So many women sat behind the locked gates.
Their souls were destroyed- they'd accepted
their fate.

As they shuffled her in, she then promised
herself,
that unless she was sickly and suffered ill health,
she would give it her all - she would fight all the
way,
for her freedom and life, and make them rue the
day.

She will rise from the ashes - her terror will
reign.
She will never be fearful of a man again.
She's ready to fight, she's ready to lead.
Expose them as frauds with their faults and their
greed.

Witchcraft they want - then witchcraft they'll
get!
With intention alone she'll make them all regret!
'Cause hell hath no fury - and she had been
scorned.
Now death was upon them - and they had been
warned....

Witch Trials - Part 2 - The First Act.

The click of the lock, the key on the chain
made her fear burn her stomach, but she had to
refrain.
She cast her eyes over the sea of despair,
their faces near frozen in desolate stare.

She noticed a figure to her left, near the door.
A dishevelled old woman laying on the cold
floor.
She made her way over, sat next to her form,
laid her coat on her shoulders to keep her skin
warm.

She was shivering with cold and consumed with
her fear,
but she sat up to focus and wipe back a tear.
"My name's Mary Sutton dear - how do you do?
I'm guessing they've beat and broken you down
too."

As she sat there with Mary, her eyes looked
around.
She heard them all scream without making a
sound.

It clicked in her mind what they needed to do,
she stood up, cleared her throat, raised her voice
loud and true.

"We have been placed here, in this holding cell.
They believe us to be evil sent here from hell.
But the secret they keep - the one they hold dear,
is the fact that we're locked up because of their
fear.

They fear us as women, it's felt by them all.
Our knowledge and wisdom makes them feel so
small.
So they deem us as spell casters, wicked, insane.
Cunning women of lore whom they need to
restrain.

Remember your power, your strength and your
worth.
We're women of soul and healers of Earth.
Stand with me as one, reclaim our divine!
Let our magick prevail and our worthiness
shine!"

A humming of chatter had now filled the room.
A unity surfaced from impending doom.
But before they devised and had worked out a
plan,

they came to collect them - and the Trial Tests
began.

"Hurry up woman!" - he yelled with disgrace,
"I'm talking to you hag, so lift up your face!"
Poor Mary, the oldest of all present here,
raised her head, met his eyes, knew her fate was
now near.

Her illness in childhood had caused her to walk,
with a limp in her gait and a click when she
talked.
The stroke left her numb, her eye sockets
displaced,
and a surgical scar from her neck to her waist.

"Ah! You are the one sent here by Donald Moor
after watching you practice plant medicine lore.
An old witch of sorcery, you cannot deny!
Your deformaties prove that you're of Evil Eye."

Dear Mary had known that it wouldn't make
sense,
to angrily scream and plead in her defence.
It's true she had wisdom of plant and herb lore,
passed down from her mother, and her mother
before.

"Our first stop today will be at the great lake,

We'll view for ourselves how much Mary can
take!"
She rushed up to Mary, held her up as she
swayed,
then processed the statement that he had just
made.

As the hatred inside of her bubbled and brewed,
her green eyes bore hate in his eyes of steel blue.
His smile curved into a sneer of sheer revolt,
a frightening expression that quickened her
pulse.

"I should have you know - and I will have you
learn,
that my name's Matthew Hopkins, and this is
John Stearne.
I'm the Witchfinder General, and with John by
my side,
we capture the witches- there's no place to
hide."

The panic created from those spoken words
proved intention of sufferance in which they'd
all heard.
"I'll tell you a tale" - he said with a grin,
"Of the fate of the witch who was burned at
Kings Lynn.

Go to the marketplace, on the wall you will see,
a heart carved in stone as reminder to thee -
that as she was screaming, engulfed in the
flames,
her heart left her body - leapt out from her
frame.
It landed intact as it hit the stonewall.
A heart carved in place as a warning to all."

The women fell silent, their mouths open wide.
The terror of how that poor woman had died!
Some screamed to have mercy, some cried out
their dread,
some reeling in disbelief from what was just
said.

"Now gather yourselves, prepare your mindset.
One chance to prove innocent- one chance you
will get.
You'll all be the first to have witnessed the
news,
Mary Sutton, first witch swum in the River
Ouse......"

Witch Trials - Part 3 - The Horrors Endured.

Recoiling in shock, Mary buckled her knees as she looked up at Matthew and cried out her pleas.
"Get up now old woman, for now it's too late to be pleading for mercy- you must face your fate!"

At the rivers edge waited an unruly crowd.
They were very impatient, their voices were loud.
"Drown the witch!" someone said. "Tie her up like a swine!
If she sinks, then she passes, if she floats... there's your sign!"

She was knocked to the ground, she was stripped of her clothes.
 A long piece of rope bound her thumbs to her toes.
"Now Mary," - said Matthew, "This water is pure.
It will spit you out, - make you float. This I am sure!

If you float you are guilty beyond reasonable
doubt.
If you sink, you are innocent and we'll help get
you out."

As the poor woman lay helpless, void of all hope
-
her body entangled and held with thick rope -
she was picked up and swiftly thrown into the
deep,
where the streambed fell into a declining steep.

The two men assigned to hold onto the ends
of the rope felt it tighten, then slacken again.
The water went back to an unbroken skin.
The silence was proof she was honest herein.

'Twas hard to know just how much time had
now passed.
It seemed that those last moments were Mary's
last.
Then all of a sudden- an almighty splash,
emerged from the depths, then she took a big
gasp.

Try as she did, she could not sink back down,
so they pulled her ashore and she fell to the
ground.

"You're a witch! You're a sorceress! Guilty as
tried!
Now you'll hang in the gallows as we all watch
you die!"

She was untied and taken to the holding cells.
Her breathing was shallow and she felt unwell.
Her lungs full of water- God knows she had
tried!
She collapsed and stopped breathing- then
suddenly died.

"You killed her! You murderer! Her blood's on
your hands!
You're the most evil sadist that ever did stand!"
The woman who spoke had not spoken before.
Her face was contorted, her eyes red and sore.

"Well, what have we here?" Matthew's voice
boomed aloud.
"Show yourself to me woman! Step away from
the crowd!"
A young woman walked to the front of them all.
He'd seen her approaching as she was so tall.

She stood over him with a threatening stance.
He thought she may strike him if she had the
chance.
He stood back to regain his power and pride,

and beckoned John Stearne to come stand by his
side.
"What is your name?" - he demanded to know.
Her voice cracked in reply, her speech heavy and
slow...

"My name is Jane Wenham." She shuffled her
feet.
She avoided his stare, hung her head in defeat.
"I believe you had bewitched a young servant
maid.
You'd said you would get justice some other
way!

Accused of witchcraft by your boss, you were
willing,
to sue defamation. Your reward was a shilling.
Not impressed with the outcome, you were
heard to say thrice,
you would bewitch a servant- make her pay the
price!

We shall search you for Witch Marks that lay on
your skin.
If we find one, you're to repent and pay for your
sins!"
A birthmark, a mole, a scar he would play -

he'd say they were Witch Marks, and she'd have
no say.

To try and deter him from making that choice,
she licked her dry lips and she then found her
voice.
"To prove I am worthy, to prove I am true,
can you swim me like Mary? Can I take that test
too?"

"You don't get to choose from the Witch Trial
tests,
you'll be given the one that we think suits you
best!
Since you've come across cocky, with graces
and airs,
We'll give you the "Prayer Test" - recite the
Lords' Prayer.
The script must be fluent and free of all errors.
If correct- we'll release you from facing your
terrors.

A witch cannot read such a biblical verse,
without mistake or error for their tongue has
been cursed!"
Jane started reciting without further ado.
It was perfect and faultless- her confidence grew.
Perhaps too much surety- as she had to contend.

She forgot a whole line - an err she could not mend.

She was hung up at midnight amidst comments of hate.
After death she was placed near the holding cell gates.
This witch had failed- beaten at her own game,
then thrown in a shallow grave that did not bare her name....

Witch Trials - Part 4 - The Realisation.

So it continued - these horrific trials that made
these women vomit and choke on their bile.
Two women were tried and forced to admit,
they'd bewitched two young children who'd
started to fit and convulse and pass out with their
fists clenched so tight!
Not a one could unclench them - try as they
might!

They made the women try - and what have you
know,
that their touch caused the stiffness to release
and let go.
They failed the "Touch Test" - which made these
women fall.
If the witch cursed that person - the curse could
be recalled.

Only the touch of the witches accused would
revert the curse, causing the spell to diffuse.
Their guilt was apparent, they were hung up
aswell.

Their bodies hung broken, their souls gone to
Hell.

A mystery illness plagued a family of four.
They'd accused Alice Samuel- as she'd
threatened before...
So they made a "Witch Cake" - a horrible eat
that consisted of ashes and rye meal, with wheat.

The final ingredient was to come from the witch.
Some of her urine thrown into the mix.
Then baked as a cake and fed to her pet,
to reveal the name guilty and repay their debt.
It wasn't a good test- as the pet would not eat,
that horrible cake they'd passed off as a treat.

"Incantations" or "charging" was a test they all
thought was the easiest way for a witch to be
caught.
If they had a victim whom they'd made
possessed,
they must call on the Devil to evoke them at
best.

Should the poor soul in trance then awake from
their state,
then that witch was to hang and accept it her
fate.

Alice was to recite a particular verse,
that evoked the bad spirits and took back the
curse.
Others were made to recite it aswell,
to prove whom had power to revoke the spell.

The others were first made to act on this test.
They recited the verse and commanded at best.
When seen that the family were still all
possessed,
they'd proved Alice guilty- as they had all
guessed.

As Alice stood standing with tears on her cheek,
she recited the verse she was then forced to
speak-
"As I am a witch, I charge the devil inside,
for this family to come out of their fits at this
time."

The family recovered, came out of their trance.
They'd found Alice guilty- she was given her
chance.
They cheered as poor Alice was beaten and
hung.
She'd exposed her own guilt with the words
from her tongue.

As the townsfolk rejoiced in the victory at hand,

Matthew's witch hunting skills were deemed
best in the land.
He and John were made heroes despite their
cruel ways.
Paid enough to retire and live out their days.

"The last tests I'd like to be trialled upon she -
whom was first to be spared and cut down from
the tree.
The woman who tried to seduce me then say,
she was trialled after I hadn't gotten my way.

Now come forth young lady, your trial will
begin.
Have haste as my patience is wearing quite
thin!"
Everybody had waited for her to appear,
as the women looked for her with faces of fear.

She didn't emerge or make herself known.
Matthew squinted his eyes- his suspicions had
grown..
He realised then, that sometime today,
She'd escaped from her captives and had gotten
away!!

Witch Trials - Part 5 - The Revenge.

She'd escaped at the time when poor Mary was
tried,
and she'd seen from a distance when Mary had
died.
Through tears of much sorrow, she'd worked out
a way,
to expose the Witchfinder and make sure he
paid.

She'd wait until dusk when the last trials were
near.
At the time least expected- her face would
appear.
She would take great delight in then hearing him
plead,
then deny him of mercy in his time of need.

He regained his composure from panicked to
poised and demanded the townsfolk to quieten
their noise.
"No doubt in my mind" - he angrily spat -
"She'll be killed by wild creatures and will not
be back.

She will meet her own destiny - fate, you will
see.
She'll endure a death suitable, as it should be!"
And with that he continued the role he had
played, to keep alive the "Witch fever" that he
had portrayed.

After briefly conversing, the two men declared,
that the next woman trialled would be Marjory
Baird.
As Marjory heard her name, she stood up, and
felt sure,
she'd be found innocent- unlike others before.

But Matthew and John were determined to find,
that she would prove guilty for her accused
crimes.
"Strip Marjory naked - a mark you shall see.
A branding from Satan that she did receive.

Once making a pact with the devil himself,
the witches are "marked" with a prominent
welt."
Marjory then knew that her battle was lost,
stripped bare of her clothes which they'd torn off
and tossed.

Across her front torso, an angry mark lay.
A mark that she'd had from her very first day.

The townsfolk had gasped - how could she
deny?
Above the loud chatter came Marjory's reply -

"This is a birthmark, this isn't a sign!"
She held her chin high and she straightened her
spine.
But no matter what poor Marjory now claimed,
her guilt was apparent- her birthmark to blame.

The townsfolk turned lynch mob was a horrific
sight,
demanding for justice as day turned to night.
"Hang the witch, tie her up," a man was heard
say.
"We should hang all the others, they're of guilt
anyway."

The women all knew that their time was now
near.
They were all to be killed - they had made that
fact clear.
The folk had turned brutal, blood thirsty,
enraged.
Their eyes spoke of evil, their faces were crazed.

Then all of a sudden, behind Matthew's back -
she'd returned shooting bullets,starting an
attack.

That maddening crowd that had wanted them
dead,
had all seen a bullet shoot straight through
John's head.

As he lay there dying, the crowd had then heard,
the guilty admissions of John's final words...

"Oh Lord, please have mercy- forgive my
partake,
in the swimming of Mary Sutton down by the
lake.
The hanging of Jane - for her death was a curse.
She'd mistakenly missed reading a line in a
verse.

The two women blamed and then forced to
admit,
they'd cursed two young children and caused
them to fit.
And poor Alice Samuel, deemed guilty by law,
for striking ill a wealthy family of four.

These women were made to look like they'd
possessed,
the workings of witchcraft, then forced to
confess.
The money we've made from this - Matthew and
I,

made us very greedy and made us both lie."

With one final gasp, he took his last breath, in a
pool of his blood where his body lay rest.
Matthew then sharply stated, "That just isn't
true!
They were guilty of witchcraft, I think John was
too!

They were killed but yet innocent! That's what
he'd said!
Sounds like he had been cursed before being
shot dead!"
She looked at him squirming, explaining his
ways.
His focus was fading, his eyes in a daze.
Nobody believed what he'd proposed of John.
The crowd disembarked and did not carry on.

"Now ladies"- she stated, "I need your advice.
Your thoughts on his punishment, and do not
think twice!
I thought it deemed fit for this hideous man,
to endure the first test in where this all began!"

They all nodded their heads in agreeance of
course.
Marched Matthew to River Ouse with much
needed force.

Bound his wrists to his ankles then thrown in the
deep -
where the streambed falls into a declining steep.

He screamed and he pleaded, and bad luck for
him that he floated, found guilty. Was tried for
his sins.
It seemed he gave up, for he then disappeared,
and did not resurface. The women all cheered.

And so was the tale of Matthew and John,
whose fates had been sealed from them both
doing wrong.
Innocent women had paid with their lives.
Shown no mercy and tortured amidst fearful
cries.

Self.

Remember- she is brave.
She knows her fears yet rises up to greet them
every day.
Acknowledge - her truths.
She looks upon her shadow and forgives
decisions made wrongly in her youth.
Forgive - her childish ways.
Sometimes retaliation heats her hot head causing
inner child to play.
Protect - her inner being.
That soul of delicate structure can be captured in
her eyes and seen.
Nourish - her intellect.
Spark interest, stimulate her love of learning.
Push through new boundaries, rise through
thought collect.
Give - her time to grow.
 Plant new experiences and life wisdom from the
seeds you sow.
Embrace - her warrior stance.
Her goddess stature, feminine power, know her
worth and feel it with a glance.
Empower - her uplifting state.
Let her gift her fellow woman, help her rise,
sisters of warm embrace.

Seduce her - fall in love.
 With who she is and what she was and who
she'll be - love all of the above.
Love her - without the rules.
Unconditional and always, never play her fool.
Stand by her - be her best friend.
Know that she is never by herself, as you stand
for her now and always, and forever, until the
end.

One moment.

He saw her. She saw him.
A smile exchanged. A passing grin.
She saw his eyes. They shared a gaze.
He saw her beauty. His thoughts had dazed.

She thought to ask - but then felt shy.
He saw her pause - he';d wondered why.
He then felt that his chance had flown.
Unspoken words, she hadn't known.

They passed each other. Time carried on.
Remaining strangers. The moment gone.
Two soul mates lost. Two hearts denied.
He went to work broken. She went home and
cried.

They'd walked past true love, and they each
never knew,
that the other was feeling the exact way too.
Too scared to reveal, and so they'd assumed.
Found and lost their true soul mate before love
had bloomed.

She Knows.

When lies are spoken
and hidden truths
contort upon the lips she once kissed -
although she doesn't show it....
She knows.

When heads are bowed
and eyes refuse to hold her stare
that once told stories of forever-
although she doesn't speak it....
She knows.

When looking at your feet
and wiping sweaty palms
of hands she thought she'd always treasure-
believe me she can feel it.....
She knows.

Don't ever underestimate
or insult her intelligence.
Cause once you've played that game,
then realise she knew-
your second chance is never...
She's gone.

Shadow.

Scry into the mirror deep.
Peer into the dark.
Truth emerged for you to keep,
once peeling back the bark.

Face the woman looking back,
don't fear her masks of many.
Observe her and the mask will crack
and show her faults if any.

Lay your triggers on the table
and dig deep to find the roots.
Then show her you are able
to ascend from hidden truths.

Confronting as it sounds to be
you must not break away.
Remember- "she's a part of me"
so understand her play.

The shadow is the traits of self
you hide from all you know.
You also hide them from yourself
when buried down below.

To know her is to love her,
understand her warts and all.
Make peace with all her faces,
watch her trip - but break her fall.

Celestial Connection.

I'd like to introduce to you -
perhaps you've known before.
Come ride a little journey to
the realm of Herbal Lore.

Behold these gifts of nature.
Abundant they do thrive.
They heal us with their spirit,
make our senses come alive.

They hold their perfect structure,
try to fault them if you dare.
Their scent alone can heal you
as their perfumes fill the air.

They each possess an antidote
to heal us without fail.
Medicinal and spiritual,
there's one for every ail.

A living organism that
can grow and reproduce.
A poultice or a tincture beneficial
from their use.

Steep as a tea and drink
their herbal remedies as well!
Place in your balms and healing salves
and in your magick spells.

Sow your own and watch them -
take some notes on how they grow.
Harvest them with love and
when you talk to them - they know!

The alchemy in nature -
sulfer, mercury and salt,
Is "mind," "spirit" "body"
and describes them without fault.

That is how they aid us,
with their healing as a whole.
Their essence as assistance
to our mind, spirit and soul.

They each have their own Zodiac
and ruling planets too!
The words of "plant" and "planet"
showing all of us a clue...

For every plant on Earth,
their characteristic traits align,
and match up with a planet
when their facets both combine.

Celestial connection that's
reflected between planes.
Our plants - the "planets,"
planets - "plants".
They're mirrored as the same.

The planes of Being and Life
connected more than we all know.
The universe connection-
"As Above, So Below."

Crystal Energies.

I am at one with nature.
I believe in the divine.
I concoct herbal remedies
and look for spiritual signs.

I work with tools of magick,
many of which I possess.
I'd like to tell you more about
the tools I work with best.

They're found to lay amongst the rocks
and creeks and riverbeds.
In sediments of sands
and even found inside your head!

The energies of crystals are
so sacred to behold.
With healing properties and magick
powers to be told.

I won't tell you about them all -
there's thousands at my guess.
So I will talk of crystals
that I've found to suit me best.

The first one - Amethyst,
the "Symbol of Sincerity."
Assists our immune system,

strengthens psychic ability.

Black Quartz stimulates the brain,
revives it - to be fair.
It creates a sense of calm
and transmutes bad vibes in the air.

Clear Quartz is very similar
and has a high demand.
When meditating it will
stimulate the pineal gland.

The "Symbol of Success and Love"
has Jade a fav of mine.
It strengthens heart and kidneys
and it radiates divine.

Can't go past the beauty of
the Lapis Lazuli.
Allows the tension to release
and help you speak your mind.

Malachite is excellent
to vitalise the soul.
Reveals subconscious blocks
and helps the body as a whole.

Moonstone is a healer -
likes to sit with Inner Child.
Possesses feminine energy
and tames emotions wild.

Rose Quartz an all time favourite.
Big love is felt when near.
Enhances love of self
and clears guilt, jealousy and fear.

Love the hues of colour
In the Golden Tiger Eye.
Enhances clear perception. Grounds.
Protects from Evil Eye.

Black Tourmaline- A great stone
that will help a sensitive being,
who may become encaptured
from discordant energies.

Zoisite (Green with Ruby),
has good grounding properties.
It benefits us greatly
in our network energy.

I have so many others,
but for now I've named a few.
Take notice when you hold them,
see what crystals work for you!

The Next Door Neighbour.

He peeked between the curtains
of his loungeroom near the door.
His tabby cat stayed sleeping,
purring loudly on the floor.

He couldn't help but watch
the women move their things inside.
His help was never offered,
friendly greetings he denied.

His neighbour sold the house
and moved away down to the coast.
His friend of 15 years had left.
The one he'd liked the most.

He didn't get along with
others living in the street.
He'd turn the other way
when they would raise their hand in greet.

And now he has to suffer,
with these women moving in.
Two sisters unlike-
for one was fat, the other thin.

The fat one was the loudest.
A wart sat on her nose.
Her feet too swollen for her shoes
exposing all her toes.

The thin one had stayed quiet.
Her beady eyes were small.
The fat one short and stocky
whilst the thin one was quite tall.

Then it had dawned upon him -
Yes, he thought this as true,
as the thin one filled a cast iron pot,
left on a fire to brew.

"I live next door to witches!"
he had gasped then gave a shout.
The fat one waved her hands
and magickally the fire went out.

The thin one had some items
she had moved out from the car.
He saw she held a broomstick
as he strained to see that far.

He watched her as she carried them
right up to the front door.
She left them there then turned around
to go and collect more.

'Twas then she noticed that her pot
of water hadn't brewed.
She then yelled at the fat one -
Cussing her, and acting lewd.

The fat one stormed outside,
she looked the thin one in the eye.
Her hand had held a cobweb
and the body of a fly.

She placed them in a jar
then sealed the top with melted wax.
The thin one looked surprised
and caught off guard from the attack.

The fat one raised her head and
said the words, "So Mote it Be."
Then took the jar and buried it
behind the apple tree.

The thin one said her sorries,
but she knew it was too late.
Her body became paralysed-
stuck in a web of fate.

Everything fell silent,
all except a weary moan,
emerging from the thin one

as her body turned to stone.

The fat one held a hammer.
With force she'd slammed it down.
The statue of the the thin one
lay in pieces on the ground.

He saw her catch her breath,
then watched in horror as she sat -
to stroke the fluffy fur of his
beloved tabby cat!

The cat ate fish and liver.
Had demolished every bite.
He gathered up his courage
and prepared himself for fight.

He walked next door to greet her.
She knew that he was there.
His tabby stayed beside her
in a trance of vacant stare.

"Are you the owner of this cat,
this handsome little boy?
That's won me over with his snuggles
bringing me such joy?"

"Yes, that is me," he'd said whilst standing
safely out the way.

"I've come to greet my tabby and
collect him if I may."

"You live there by yourself? she asked.
"Just you and tabby cat?"
"That's us," he said, picked tabby up
and started to walk back.

"I live here by myself aswell,
gets lonely I must say.
I'd love some company to spend some time
and fill my days."

Of course she didn't know
he'd seen the thin one die alone.
She'd paralysed her body,
turned her structure into stone.

He cleared his throat then stated,
"I'm quite busy, I'll have you know.
I'm hardly ever home and I am always on the
go.
I may not have the time to have a chat or say
gidday,
so please don't think I'm making an excuse to
stay away."

"So busy," she repeated.
"Yet you had the time to peek!

I saw you standing, watching us,
you've snooped on us all week!!

I know you saw what happened
to my sister here before.
Your fate will be like hers
if you don't come knock on my door!"

He visited her often.
Bought her cakes and lots of sweets.
Made her lovely dinners, brewed her teas and
cooked her treats.

So that's how it had started -
this friendship of the two.
Born out of fear and blackmail.
No one ever had a clue.

Feminine Elements.

She's Fire - Impulsive and Courageous.
Difficult to silence.
Speaks her mind and triumphs.
Hot tempered and holds beauty.

She's Earth - Practical and Grounded.
Sensual, Connected.
Deep in her perfection.
Logical and Lovely.

She's Air - Intelligent and Social.
Curious and Vocal.
Peaceful and Approachable.
Balanced in her Grace.

She's Water - Emotional and Fluid.
Nurturing and Complex.
Goddess of a Woman.
Empathetic- holding space.

Together- They are Spirit.
The link between the realms.
Connecting body to the soul.
Feminine becomes whole.

Different.

Oh why, my beautiful child?
Why did you replace
your unique self with normal?
Dim the light that shines your face?

You stood out for a reason.
Weren't in that shade of grey.
You radiated colour
life abundant and at play.

You erased all the sparkle.
The glittered flecks of gold.
Drew shadows all around you,
to help you fit the mould.

You learnt to stoop your shoulders,
to stay hidden in the crowd.
You used to stand so straight and tall,
you used to feel so proud.

So tell me, gentle creature.
Do tell me angel soul,
Of why you'd made decisions
to remove yourself as whole?

And in your place stands nothing
but a shell that bears your face.
Lost your smile, dimmed your light.
You walk a slower pace.

Don't dull your soul to fit in/
be accepted as "the norm."
Your light can't guide the others
if you camouflage your form.

You have a high vibration and
a happy warm embrace.
A smile to gift to others
when it's glowing on your face.

Don't ever dim your light to fit
into the "normal" crew.
You're made to vibrate differently
when you choose to be you. Xx

Dark of Night.

The night became their saviour.
They wore its cloak of black.
The outcasts of society
were never coming back.

The two of them were similar,
yet so different all the same.
They'd be there for the other one
if they had cried their name.

They trusted next to no one.
Relied on not much help.
Went tumbling through life and
played the cards they had been dealt.

There wasn't a thing wrong with them
as far as they could tell.
Yet teachers just ignored them
and their classmates had all yelled.

But in the cloak of darkness
they were like everyone else.
Were treated with respect
which then made them respect themselves.

The two became nocturnal.
Safe in their comfort womb.
They danced around a fire,
told their secrets to the moon.

Dreamstate.

I dreamt of happy memories, times of popularity.
I thought that equalled happiness.
Turned out it wasn't so.

I won the local lottery,
had millions of dollars, went overseas.
I thought I could buy happiness.
The answer screamed out no.

Awarded increased salary.
Looked at my pay check- couldn't see
the reason why I did agree.
The hours killed me though.

I dropped the ball, stepped out from the
illusion of normality,
Looked back and saw some parts of me
weren't coming where I'd go.

They stayed behind, I didn't miss
the old - it just failed to exist,
creating a new life of bliss
to satisfy my soul.

And guess what? Oh

could you have guessed?
I finally found happiness,
by breaking free from troubled stress
I'm now completely whole.